THE INCENTIVE OF THE MAGGOT

The
INCENTIVE
of the MAGGOT

Poems

Ron Slate

A Mariner Original / Houghton Mifflin Company

Boston   New York

For information about permission to reproduce
selections from this book, write to Permissions,
Houghton Mifflin Company, 215 Park Avenue South,
New York, New York 10003.

Visit our Web site: www.houghtonmifflinbooks.com.

Library of Congress Cataloging-in-Publication Data
Slate, Ron.
    The incentive of the maggot : poems / Ron Slate.
       p.   cm.
    "A Mariner original."
    ISBN 0-618-54358-9
    I. Title.

    PS3619.L365I53   2005
    811'.6 — DC22   2004060947

Book design by Melissa Lotfy

Printed in the United States of America

QUM 10 9 8 7 6 5 4 3 2

For my wife, Nancy Gilson,
for our children, Abigail, Jenny, and Stacey,
and for all who remember Lester Gilson

CONTENTS

III.

FOREWORD

Poetry that is "better than the movies": Ron Slate's *The Incentive of the Maggot* meets that challenge, tossed by Frank O'Hara in his mock manifesto, "Personism." Slate understands that art must first of all (as O'Hara's predecessor Henry James requires) be interesting. *Inter est:* what is between or among, as in "financial interest" or "shared interest" or "national interest."

And the interesting fact of nations appears in the first section of this book, where titles include "Writing Off Argentina," "Belgium," "Small Talk in Munich," and "The Plan for Cyprus." Conventional expectation is for poetry to deal with political, historical material as a matter of sensibility: with rhetoric more than thought, with slogans rather than complexity. When it comes to politics, the poet may be expected to take righteous, easy attitudes — against atrocity and in favor of peace, just like the politicians.

These poems are the opposite: muscular, ironic, informed. Slate's characteristic movement is a quick, nervous progress away from the superficial, through erratic reversals and subversions, toward a rediscovery of the starting point, transformed. That arc, the course from innocence to serpentine consideration, reflects an attraction of Slate's work: these are distinctly the poems of an adult.

For instance, any sophomore might quote a political figure's joke. "Belgium" opens:

> Invented by the British to annoy
> the French, so said De Gaulle.
> The Belgians are rude but live to please.

But this little formula evolves into the motif for variations on the theme of power, need, the conduct of nations and people: peace among western nations "to annoy the Chinese"; Belgium as a battleground in 1915, needing help to feed its eleven million people; Herbert Hoover heading the relief effort and believing in an elite of "uncommon men"; contemporary Brussels as a theater for international law where, as "uncommon men," diplomats come

> for reassurance, each voice will be heard,
> each nation will achieve the goal
>
> of living off all the other nations.
> A relation of men dominating men.
> Now it's your turn, now mine.
>
> The guards take a look under the limo
> and wipe for traces of ill intent.

A first-person element threads through the poem: early on, "We dress for dinner / but the ambassador dresses down"; then, near the end, "I sign the guest book." The terms of manners — "annoy" and "rude" in De Gaulle's little quip and the succeeding line — first appear as a joke about nations, as though they behave on the same level as individuals. Then the poem takes another view, in which the levels of individuals and nations are not so easy to separate, their joining not so absurd: signing the guest book, bearing ill intent and wiping for traces of it are individual actions in one way but in other ways dictated by global forces. Conversely, nations compete and struggle like "common men."

This first group of poems brings together the personal and the global in a way that is distinctive, subtle, defying expectations about what is political and what is personal. Cultural meanings and symbols shift unreliably, eroding the sense of individual destiny. In "End of the Peacock Throne," the New Year's symbol of a rose, printed in a newspaper, is read by the shah's secret police as a coded insult, occasion for arrest and torture; in "The Plan for Cyprus," a concert of players who "come in neither peace nor war" makes the idea of neutrality seem not merely hopeless but perhaps corrupting to the players.

That first section prepares the way for a book that is increasingly intimate in feeling, even in occasional detail, without conventional moves of autobiography or first-person lyric. The title poem, for instance, resists clichés of personal narrative, just as the first poems in the volume resist clichés of global perspective. The introductory scene is of young nurses summoned to observe a severe case of gangrene, apparently accelerated by anti-infection medication. That situation — the nurses who study the terrible wound, the uncurable dilemma that the medication for one problem exacerbates another problem, the mechanical, fallible attempt at instructive *looking* — is another little tune that will snake through its variations and complexities:

> They make them look
> at the uncurable, and struggle with the sense
> of regimen, while we in the waiting room
>
> wait for outcomes and the screen flashes
> with the image of a small plane crashing,
> then crashing again in slow motion,
>
> a privately owned twin-engine tilting
> at the runway cleared for its return.
> Overheated room, everyone is nodding off.
>
> Insurgents shot in Sri Lanka and Liberia.
> Bones found nearby in the Neponset marshes.

The patients in the waiting room cannot be blamed for dozing through various horrors on the TV news; then we are startled by returning to the nurses, but also to an implied poetics — or is it an ethics? — that is suspicious of spectacle:

> So a young nurse, of a particular temperament,
>
> may come to resent, may angrily refuse
> to use grief for the purpose of edification.
> She may feel contempt for a journalist's catalogue

of atrocities, genitals beaten with a ruler.
Not because they are not actual,
but because someone looked and discovered nothing.

Then, abruptly, Josephus's description of Herod the Great suffering with gangrene: "The brains behind / the Slaughter of the Innocents died of gangrene / in his penis." Then another unexpected, abrupt twist back to the television news, but to what is forbidden to be looked at:

But we will not have to look at the coffins

of our dead soldiers. They will not let us
gaze on their coffins, in transit.
Praise for the edict that will not permit

videotape to roll over the suddenly dead.
Praise for this moment of pause, of darkness.

The power here is not simply in the ironic "praise" but in the doubling back that teases complacency: like the theoretical nurse who objects to the voyeuristic, bland catalogue of atrocities, the repressive government officials are on the side of not seeing something repellent, though for radically different reasons. And the unseen coffins are in some ways more instructive than the bones in Neponset or the plane visibly crashing again and again in slow motion.

This resembles the doubleness of the infection-fighting drugs that as a side effect "encourage the gangrene." But the idea of the destructive cure is itself reversed in the closing lines:

Not long ago I sat with a clairvoyant;

she said in my past life
I was slain on an English battlefield.
But others were saved by green blowflies,

their larvae made a soup in the gashes and rips,
dressed the wounds and farmed our flesh.
The survivors lay in a drowse of pain.

Timelessly they stirred, rose up, staggered in boots
and quickened their steps, as if they had discarded
the dead parts of themselves.

This is a tormented as well as bold meditation on ambiguities of corruption and survival, of witnessing and ignoring, of instruction and oblivion. The scale of disorder and the tortuous reversals —infections that preserve, larvae that heal—are commensurate with Slate's resolve to keep these irresolutions not merely paradoxical but urgent: measures of difficulty.

The poems afford the valuable pleasure of arriving at the unexpected by unpredictable routes. "The klaxons save us by startling," says the first line of "Safe Passage," and there's something like an implied *ars poetica* in the line. Here are American poems in which political forces are imagined with passion and understanding, accorded all the resistant and astonishing density of the real.

—ROBERT PINSKY

I

WRITING OFF ARGENTINA

This morning the peso is free-floating
above the unstable world of Borges.

He knew Buenos Aires was not a city
to die in. Geneva was that much closer

to the other world. When the system fails
the theory of the system becomes pure

and the housewives of Buenos Aires gather
outside Congress and bang their pots and pans,

and their husbands gather outside the courthouse
and jangle their car keys, proudly to ask,

What have you done to our good life?
Brazilian joke: Why do Argentines run outdoors

when there's lightning? Because they think God
is taking their photograph.

Borges asked, What man has never felt
that he has lost something infinite?

When the economy falls apart, you feel that loss,
plus your pesos deflate to illustrate.

Yesterday on the Avenida Borges, we lived
in this world, but what were we like?

We took our dollars to buy leather coats
at the shop of Esteban Umansky,

who gave each of us a hat and gloves.
The president himself attended

our reception, and the ex-president,
now under house arrest for the millions

in his Swiss account. So the Argentines
go to Switzerland to hoard and die,

and we go to Buenos Aires to shop and live.
When Borges went to Geneva to die

the Argentines thought it was some kind
of poetic conceit. They were too cocky to see

he had given up trying to express himself.
Something great had been lost, some treasure.

He had decided all men are benighted.
This morning of the wrecked and plundered

I am all-seeing but my soul is blind.
I feel very much like myself.

In pursuit of a deal in leather,
in pursuit of one's money in the shuttered banks,

we are forgetting how to be decently unhappy.
Learn from the global lenders, writing off

their bad Argentine debts. Their dual wisdom:
First, understanding the loss. Then,

understanding there's nothing to be done.
I understand and I love my odorous coat

and Esteban made me a jacket as well
at a price not to be believed.

THE FINAL CALL

Is this the end of the world?
No, just the end
of the language that describes it.

So the end happens
but no one says anything.
It's a downturn, not a collapse,

an economist explains.
The pair of polite apostles ringing
my doorbell are in no rush to die.

In the literature of the last days
there are many typos.
Dead, dread, bread, take your pick.

Whoever is saying it's over
refuses to specify demands,
makes no ultimatums, it's just over.

What kind of language is that?
Analysts are antic with interpretation,
think tanks are flooding with thoughts.

The global information network
backs up the data, streams it up
to one of Jupiter's moons.

The ram's horn heralds
our coming from the hills.
We're enslaved by that sound.

We're called to hang-glide
from hilltops into the open air
where we verify and counterpunch.

Ah, another soft landing.
Though this time a rather large sheet of sky
tangles and trails down after us.

BELGIUM

Invented by the British to annoy
the French, so said De Gaulle.
The Belgians are rude but live to please,

live by pleasing. Speaking languages.
Renting their houses.
They're not rude, they just drive that way.

We dress for dinner
but the ambassador dresses down.
The western nations don't understand each other.

Never to go to war with one another again.
Invented by the western nations
to annoy the Chinese.

Our ambassador dresses down.
It's his wife's birthday.
Staff of eight lives to please.

Herbert Hoover saved Belgium in 1915
with seven million tons for eleven million.
Saved Belgium from Germany and England

who misunderstood each other.
Hoover believed in uncommon men.
The ambassador is an uncommon man.

He and others come to Brussels
for reassurance, each voice will be heard,
each nation will achieve the goal

of living off all the other nations.
A relation of men dominating men.
Now it's your turn, now mine.

The guards take a look under the limo
and wipe for traces of ill intent.
The European conscience is as clean as Antarctica.

Tiny pyramids of chocolate,
a dollop of chocolate inside.
We undress for bed, the ambassador

puts on his tuxedo pants, for fit.
I sign the guest book in the morning:
First it was your time to please.

Next time it's mine.

SMALL TALK IN MUNICH

My father said find out
if his bombardier was any good.
The bombs tumbled to the spot
where I lay in a hotel bed in distress
with fever, nausea, indigestion.

Two bottles of water were delivered.
Leave them by the door.
But you must sign this receipt, sir.
Thus I signed, marking
the end of the twentieth century.

A bomb falls in no hurry,
thinking of something loud to say.
Like the businessman in the Ratskeller
listening to the waitress describe the desserts.

The twentieth century falls through the mind
in no hurry to reach a conclusion.
Plummets or spirals without expecting
to strike what it aims at.
But strikes it anyway.

Perhaps you expect madmen
mumbling in the Odeonsplatz about the ruins?
No, they're washing dishes in the Ratskeller.
In this century plates were produced
so surpassingly it was natural

to smash them and begin again,
stacking them higher and cleaner than ever.

My father's B-17 knocked down Munich
such that reassembly was possible.
A spiteless city without consolation.
Germans don't make small talk
with strangers per guidebook.

The taxi driver went 140 kilometers per hour
on the autobahn but wasn't in a hurry.
I closed my eyes for the ride to the airport.
The bombardier looked down from his visionless height
and vomited, and then felt a lot better.

THE DEMISE OF CAMEMBERT

I remember my mother squeezing
the camembert. She bought it five days

before unwrapping it, unwrapped it
two hours before she served it.

But what the French sociologist calls
la déstructurisation of family meals

means there's no more patience
for ripening on the cold shelf.

This message comes to us
on a tray with quick-serve cheddar puffs

passed across the cocktail party,
across news networks via satellite.

Also it lands thudding with the flat bread,
bean salad, raisins, fruit bar,

seedless jam and plastic cutlery
in the humanitarian airdrop.

Pah! A man rejects the bland cheese couplets.
And the premoistened serviette.

In this world he fears annihilation.
This world has made him a nihilist.

Now he sits on a bed, on the bedspread
in a motel on the edge of Las Vegas

or a hotel near Narita Airport,
eating an engineered salty snack,

planning deaths designed his way,
getting more and more thirsty.

So hear me. Compassion begins in the pasture.
Adoration of cow breed, grass strain,

the certain season for milking,
the way the curd is cut and pressed

and salted and cured and shaped,
the time and temperature at each stage.

The marketing man from Coeur-de-Lion,
the number-one brand of camembert,

is revising the résumé of his ripe life.
And you and I, paring away the rind,

do you and I have a patient nose
for the creamy inwardness of things?

CROW MENACE IN TOKYO

"What will you do
when you and the whole world
are destroyed by heat?"

The Zen master sits on a tatami
in the Tenryuji Temple near Kyoto
with a brazier for hot water,

tea utensils, and a bottle
of expensive Japanese whiskey.
His face is unremarkable, unsolvable.

Yes there can be heaven on earth
but just a patch of it, a temple
or a tea room or a garden

in the Roppongi district of Tokyo
with shaded paths, ponds, flowering shrubs,
artfully untended specimen trees

and a towering building when you look up
unprepared for attack.
Also above are the crows

to be eradicated, unnaturalized.
Emboldened they peck at people.
As the twenty-five thousand crows convulse

there's a brutal heavenly brushstroke
in the sky over the little patches called Japan.
It's decorative, it's not mystical,

it's what the Zen master points to
as the answer to his *koan.*
It's a wonderful evasion of similar people

with an instinct to stay
out of trouble. Nevertheless, they understand
extremists are flying in from Islamabad.

The fullness of life is an emptiness.
The crows melt in black heat.
They'll handle the others on the hot tarmac.

END OF THE PEACOCK THRONE

Three million Iranian exiles
watch election returns on TV.
They recall pistachios and roses,
especially roses, the scented history of gardens
drifting back to the tended tomb of Cyrus.
It used to be a public life
but now it's a provisional diaspora
since whatever takes place quickly
is impermanent. Commanding his statue
to be carved in Egypt, Darius allowed
the bas-relief to betray its origins:
A Persian ruled the Nile. London
to Los Angeles, the exiles phone each other.
Do you remember, there was a poet
named Red Rose who insulted the shah.
New Year's Eve, the newspaper
printed a Persian rose beside the masthead.
Happy New Year! is what three million saw.
Death to the Shah! is what SAVAK saw
tucked in the folds of the rose.
Welcome to Komiteh Prison, Mr. Rose,
may we please have your thumbs?
My friend Hamid designed the paper.
Streaming through the global network
comes a superseding life, a pleasant tradition.
The amity of princes and presidents
is not to be trusted, susceptible to fancy.
Before Alexander burned Persepolis, he packed
10,000 mules and 5,000 camels with treasure.
Three million say: What a familiar shade of red
in this dusk, it reminds me of . . .

While Princess Leila Pahlavi watches TV,
she takes one pill for each of the 22 years
since her father lost the throne.
How the pestilence made him wilt.
Indecisive about what's pure,
in Tehran the powers issue and rescind.
As they tally and report the votes,
Princess Leila takes one pill
for each of the monarchy's 2,700 years.
Hamid claims the rose is inarticulate, innocent.
All the way to Milan, he rushed
to obtain the original artwork, to prove it.
They trailed him through airports.
He says, The rose is known by its scent,
not by what the florist or senator says.
Life is the keeping of a single breath.
With a final glottal gasp, Princess Leila dies
between two annihilations:
the time before the garden
was imagined, and the time after.

ASTRIDE THE MERIDIAN

One foot east, one foot west.
The lived life, and the other one.

On the boat ride to Greenwich
the tour guide tells a comical history.

To exit one must walk past him
and a champagne bucket clattering with coin,

the tips he earns for this entertainment,
his breath reeking of time.

In the lived life there's time,
and in time nothing happens twice,

so on each trip the story repeats
differently. Nobody is as bored

as the teller of this history
since we pay him, and money buys time,

and time repeats monotonously,
London to Greenwich and back.

Time repeats, but not the things that occur
in the lived life, and the other one

where time appears like a space with a fretted wake
behind, and Clio, muse of time, waving in the prow.

No time had been allotted to watch
the launch tape over and over again

so the space shuttle disintegrated
into flaming streaks on a family video.

The meridian is a power cable ticking,
but before it was a very long and narrow space,

a shallow niche in the flank of the planet
filled with the rubbish of conquest.

Back then, space still mystified.
Hitler, employing Greenwich time, tried

to bomb Greenwich, but there was too much space.
Now only time remains to enthrall.

If one stands astride the meridian, importunate
with history, the lived life may receive a jolt.

On the ride back to London, the river
may give off instants of glinty light.

THE PLAN FOR CYPRUS

We will assemble an orchestra,
both sexes in tuxedos.
Handsome with adequate skill,
willing to travel, and skeptical.

The logo of our sponsor will snap
in the wind above the stage.
To marvel at our mission
is to salute the courage of commerce.

We will play in the neutral zone
where it narrows to a rutted field,
Cypriot shooters on either side
running low on cigarettes.

Planes overhead will tug banners:
MACEDONIA IS AND ALWAYS WILL BE GREEK
and TURKEY GATEWAY TO PARADISE.
Up there Nicosia will look whole.

Expressly for the event
the UN will unearth the mines
and put them back when we've gone,
impartial in this affair.

Will you still call this a stunt
when oboes occupy the buffer zone?
When we levitate in links and tails
and the united dead say *ooh* and *ah*?

We will come in neither peace nor war.
We will come to make a spectacle.
Our guests will enter the safety zone
escorted through a gallery

of Greek and Turk atrocities.
The one has never been to the other side
nor will he on that night.
Our guests will be flown in excitedly.

The Greek and Turk will hear the sound.
A tune with joy in the title.
But our guests will be propelled
beyond the political, to understand

in this resisting nether land
our present and bodiless orchestra
in the middle has risked its soul,
has become a song too strange to die.

II

THEY CALLED ME

They called me Child
of the Safe Place,
the one who knows a Packard
is not a Pontiac,

the one singing to yellow
records, the naive handprint
on the new sidewalk, the one spelling

his name with a stick. They called me
what we came here for.

They called me a kidder
like his grandfather, beamish boy
after sweetwine blessings,
the boy telling scatty stories
in our accent about the war,
the boy underground, damaging at night.

They called me our banner
which is also a cape and shield,
our talking boy, learner of facts,

our extract of ear-shape, nose-shape,
the way of stepping on the train,
of being hidden in the rampancy
of a half-century's tangle of grapevines,
concertina wire, piano wire.

Our young man whom we will tell
about the used-up places. Our betrayer,

the one who saw a falling leaf turn
into a prop jet lowering to Logan,

who commands the heirlooms to line up at daybreak,
confiscates the famous recipes
because a generation of exiles is decomposing

like a lapsed anthem. The sheets snapping.
The slumped fender of the Plymouth.

They called me History with Sideburns.
They called me About to Occur.

SHAME
after Pessoa

I miss things that meant nothing to me,
and so much was nothing.
The world begins returning
like a sailor climbing the hill
to his house, lugging a duffel
bulging with what really happened.

As if the leaves aren't falling
in your mind. As if your memories
aren't like bright leaves falling,
so that the sidewalks are there
only because they are remembered
under the leaves, and things not remembered
are reshaped and unsaved.

I labor to defend myself
against the tedium of the telephone
and its cries of uncaring delight.

These dreams, these visions,
what a vulgar way to be released.
But the squeak of my office chair
is no better, the static of admonition
on the public address system.

My coworker says, The nice thing
about all this is you can't miss
what you can't remember.
Suppose you had Alzheimer's.
You'd stare at the phone
and it would mean less than nothing.

Shame of the insensate rushed hour.
Immobilized in spurts on the way home,
I miss my knitted sweater,
I miss my grandmother.
Then I climb the hill
with leaves layering the driveway
and the structure of maples candidly clear.

WHEN I RETURNED

All summer words were called out,
Grandfather groaning *My pills.*
Conductors losing patience
trackside at Lugano, Milan.
At the hotel in Locarno, I played
drums, my cousin Georges played piano,
the manager shouted *Stop this now!*

I returned home resenting
my grandfather's angina. My grandmother
yelled back at him *Don't we take care of you?*
Georges, diabetic, claimed *trafficator*
is the true English word for car directionals.
He bled when he blew his nose.

On French TV someone was interviewing
General Henri Navarre, all too successful
in having drawn out the elusive Vietminh.
I returned having eaten
in a Vietnamese restaurant, flaming
bananas. The street was blocked by students
at the American embassy, chanting
the essentials of existentialism.

In the sixties it was as if the killings
were arranged for the archives,
the cameras, unaccustomed to such access,
were loaded and attentive, the shutter barked
My God I'm hit! I came back unable to tell
the difference between my grandfather
and a president in pain in the street.

Back home, shots came from the campanile
because of symbolism and photogenics.
A man in the Place de la République
offered me a cigarette and asked me
to come down to the pissoir.
Someone called *Leave the boy alone!*
A man in the Tuileries spit at me,
Your madras jacket is stupid!

They took me to hear Claude Luter
play clarinet in a jazz club.
When I returned, I made them listen
to the words I'd learned: *"Mood Indigo,"*
nitroglycerine, Dien Bien Phu.

LIGHT FINGERS

Feather duster in a child's grip
swished over bottles of Old Grand-Dad
in my father's liquor store,
my hand hovering briefly
above rolls of coin in the cash drawer,

other objects stolen from local merchants —
a magnifying glass,
a hi-lo thermometer, an Indian rubber baseball,
novelties, candy, cigarettes:

If you wouldn't give me what I deserved,
what you seemed to promise,
then I would take it from you.
The splendor of scissors.
The consideration of a rubber stamp
"for your attention."

At some point, after the accumulation
of the objects of desire,
and later, after they became unforgettable,
beyond understanding and useless,

this is when I looked back and saw the boy
making a daring effort to be part
of the family's sadness.

All of the grief that preceded me —
war, fire, the destruction of culture,
the powerlessness of parents,
the compensations of shameful inward lives —

this, I perceived, is simply what it means
to be human. So now there is nothing
to wrest into myself,
for myself.
But there is the spirit leaping with dread

and exultation, demanding everything.
And the old cunning.

When Mrs. O'Brien suggested that Joseph,
her son, and I go to see his priest
about our common venal behavior,
my mother, a Holocaust survivor,
threw her out of the house.

I returned to my favorite pastime:
a book of sleight-of-hand tricks,
small objects, all objects, vanishing.

AFTER LONG SILENCE

Seawater spurted from my mouth.
Those who rushed to rescue me
were repelled by the smell,
we were so far from the sea.

I realized it would be pointless
to seek a new beginning
within myself.

It would be poor judgment
to make allowances for what blurts out
at any occasion and works
that sound into a sensation.

Perhaps I should have been grateful
for having been saved, should have expressed it.
Instead I revolted them by insisting

I'm a sea-creature and not a man
breathing with difficulty
and I was born on an island,
barely cresting, then swamped, then reappearing.

This time, I can't say why,
I decided to make use of this delusion.
I decided to exploit it.

But it would be foolish to think
I could begin anew.

The places I had traveled to,
they became flags of my liberty.

All the different qualities of light
one discovers in the course of a summer
living beside the bay —
I discovered my past in many lights.

Once I fumed at my own silence,
incapable of employing it.
Now I produce the unexpected sound
of something tangled in your hedge
after a wild tide.
Your supper, the ravished shell,
music, and then the amorous body.

I thought, Yes, I can make use
of the catastrophe of my past.
The part of me that had suffered
turned out to be the minor part.
The major part lay in shallow water, dredgeable,

the credible sorted from the useless
that always rushes into the net.
Give me a small and sonorous engine,
a modest wake to the island.

And of the sound
I am beginning to make —
it also reminds me of shucked shells being dumped,

the sea taking advantage any way it can,
taunting,
and not caring how things conclude.

HERMAPHRODITE ENDORMI

Hermes the Whisperer, master of sweet nothings,
spent one night with Aphrodite.

She was flattered. She had gone to Paphos
to renew her virginity in the sea.

The child was a dual-sexed being.
The child is what happens

when duality is discarded
explains the expert in the androgynous.

See the figure perfect in marble,
fingers missing on the left, one finger

and a thumb tip on the right,
otherwise an exquisite young lady,

diminutive, asleep on a cushion, sheet tossed.
Except for the penis, the tip

like the dome of a tiny Pantheon
just emerging from the foreskin.

The slightest arousal of a dream.
We came to gaze on what may resolve

into one body, for permission
to gaze. How intently we observed,

so willing to believe in a clashless life,
to be more than one thing or the other.

WARM CANTO

I don't know how to behave
in the face of ultimate things.
It's the kind of ignorance that creates
a sound, like a blind prehistoric fish
that hums to the passing of an ocean storm.
Les died four months ago, tired of emotion.
We talked to him separately
but he was gone in the warmth of the drip.
Today at 100 degrees the smell
of burned grass sharpened because I watered
the yard uselessly, invoking the essence.
The dragonfly is the enemy of the mosquito
and veers at first slowly
with wiry wrath, then again slowly.
His wings fan the fire,
the mosquito crackles into flame.
Everybody knows what a noncombustible world
would look like, everybody knows the thing
privately feared isn't private at all
but a common insect on a recurring flight.
Lester's hand was as light as a nest.
Bad news, there is no quality
of life. The drugged body of a dying man
drinks its own urine. My body grieved
that such a shock of watching should enter me.
Right up my spine, into consideration.
The mosquito in the shadow
of the dragonfly is already part of the dragonfly.
The wingbeat is a murmur of not knowing
how to behave otherwise.
Darting, the dragonfly lives. The heat kills
the reverie that kills the real.

ESSENTIAL TREMOR

We were beguiled
by four glasses of champagne
gently juddering on the table
on the Eurostar speeding through Normandy.

I had taken my daughter's photograph
at number 18 Boulevard Magenta
as my mother had asked, where she once lived.
On the way to la Gare du Nord.

On the sidewalk across the street
my grandfather stood in the crowd, in 1942,
watching Germans and gendarmes
lift his furniture into a truck and drive away.
For years he scoffed at their bad taste.

The Germans shook things up:
"Paris will now be on Berlin time."
A mantel clock was loaded on a truck,
accidentally broken, then deliberately shaken.

We were reaching top speed under the Channel
and they told me I was trembling,
holding my glass of champagne.
My cousin, a doctor, said, "It's not Parkinson's,
it's familial, it's not present
at rest or during sleep,
it barely makes a difference

except that we worry about it."
So it was true, I was slightly shaking,
filling out the immigration form.

One night, in the haven of his apartment
at Presidents Arms, on Presidents Lane,
just a block from the Adams Mansion,
my grandfather, exasperated, conceded,
"There's no restitution. It's finished."

The train emerged at Folkestone.
My daughter examined her hands.
My cousin said, "We call it essential tremor."

My mother's medications made her shake.
When John Kennedy was killed,
she interrupted my whimpering to say,
"Now you understand what they do to people."

GRANITE CITY

City hospital on one hill,
city dump on the other. Heat lightning
strafed the night between them.
The hospital smokestack blinked like a boy
agape at his first car crash.

House of my parents, ambulances
sped by with three blocks to go.
My grandparents walked home arm in arm
after dinner, Allied armies falling in
with textbooks and racing forms.

The war was over, the enemy lived on.
August came, plums turned purple
in the market, but only the red ones pleased me.
My great-aunts cleared customs, bundled
with gifts and smelling of Europe.

Terraces of granite rose from the sea.
On the heights each watery quarry had a name
and a legend, atomic creatures, gangland
graves, a kid who dived and disappeared in 1959
but died in Quang Tin from a punji spike.

When we got to the quarry, our towels rolled, the police
were taking names. Someone was missing.
Would you like a bowl of cold borscht,
asked my grandmother, listening to my story.
Beet-red, sour cream swirled it out of plasma.

History begins with indignation
because it's so hard to remember
what's been remembered. Sarcophagus
of John Adams in the First Parish Church.
His wife and son in stone beside him.

Divers failed to find the body in the blind fathoms.
It was a girl, someone shoved her.
The father asked the city to pump it out.
Curbstones, gravestones, churches, all cut
from that hole filled with rainwater.

SAFE PASSAGE

The klaxons save us by startling,
the flashing traffic gates swing down.

We are stopped on the Fore River Bridge
by the bridgekeeper, working his controls

in homage to the freighter *Prudencia,*
seaworthy after shipyard repairs.

I have stopped seeking everything
I once looked for, I am stopped

by tugboats towing out their client
through the uplifted panels.

The boat's passengers lean on a railing
and look up, men smoking in undershirts,

women and children waving. And looking down
on us from his turret, as if this moment

were his doing alone, is the bridgekeeper.
My memory is more intrigued

by what never happened than what did,
just as on this durable July evening

to idle here is never to arrive,
to want nothing more than to sense the loss

in this unforeseen lapse. The gladness heard
in the crank and slam of the bridge restored

is the strength discovered in the heart
against the grim inertia of its moving parts.

III

APPARITION OF THE VIRGIN

If there's a crack of thunder
without an attending rumble,
a great man is about to die.
If, in your dream, your clothes are flecked
with mud, or if a plant speaks to you,
expect days when love inhabits you
but is not apparent in the world,
even as others pause to let you pass,
attempting to be visible in your presence.
When the main god is a martyr, the world
is in pain. We're mirthful
in the bistro, tasting each other's dinners
since we suspect the taste of our own.
Later we drive to get a good look
at the apparition of the Virgin.
She's appearing in a window at the hospital,
moisture trapped between panes. We can clearly see
the baby in her arms, the folds of her robe,
the hem indistinct with dirt.
Along the foundation of the wall, prayers.
Please make my parents stop fighting.
Please save the missing children.
If you dream of rain, and on awaking it is August,
expect days of wine that create visions.
The grapes are swelling beyond themselves.
Expect images wavering in the rising cisterns.
But we're the things in motion, materializing,
arriving on the scene with reporters.
There is so much traffic at the hospital,
they drape the window until evening.

She is holding a hidden god in her arms,
we can clearly see he is just suggesting himself.
He is hidden in the world, so too in humans.
But we want to find, to delight
in the moist image, to depend on it.
A surgeon stares into the viscera.
A radiologist peers at a spot.
We must make way for the cutting and healing.
No matter, during off hours,
we stare at the curtain.

MONUMENTS

The green of an ancient ginkgo
outside the window of my hotel room,
the shaping pleasure of it, is a kind
of stupefaction and forgetfulness.

Some savior worried it from China
to Belgium, signifying an unfulfilled mission,
then selected an auspicious site, in 1730.
This congeries of shadings does nothing

for the imagination, but the mass
of the tree, this is more like a truth,
a full measure only now possible
to weigh, a waste of years only now known.

After millions died in the trenches,
there was a resurrection of symbols,
a flaring up of language for mourning.
On November 11 at 11 A.M.

the British would observe a two-minute silence,
moment of armistice, seconds running out
on a squalid peace, memory like transpiration
rising into gray currents above the Channel.

And the monuments, two figures of stone
at the German war cemetery at Roggevelde,
on their knees, the father hugging himself,
the robed mother's arms wrapping her body,

people of penumbral grays and too much caring.
Some critic called Käthe Kollwitz a narcissist
for using her own countenance where meaning
was heaviest and obvious. And finding only

one emotion there, ever, the etched self-portraits
becoming more somber, until at the end
she looked away from the living,
became monumental. She who opened a fatal breach

for her son, betrayed by a sense of calling,
the corrupt world calling from a pocked field
twenty kilometers northeast of Ypres,
ten days after waving goodbye.

In her diary, *The naturalistic folds*
disgust me and the stylized folds disgust me,
only the silhouette matters, more technique
than I possess. Detail accumulates, restorations

appear everywhere, but the sites of memory
somehow diminish. The French called
their disabled men *gueules cassées,*
broken faces, horrifically hurt.

They performed as shunted sites of memory,
immovable when encountered, chiseled.
When the next war began, November 11
meant nothing. When it was over,

my mother steamed artichokes, on Saturday
sat deafened under a hair dryer, then wept
on Sunday watching documentaries.
I began a long, unsuccessful attempt

to live a life in secret, with a fatal threat
of my own making — only in safety can one be
so free and meticulous in selecting one's demons.
Thus I'm reminded why I abandoned

art: disgusted with my imagination.
It occurred to Kollwitz suddenly — her face
would be the face of the mother.
The body would be trussed in grief.

We would be fictive kin to her gesture.
To nurse a sapling, westbound and eager
for renewal, to take all necessary steps,
make the pilgrimage, and then fail

to achieve the inner experience —
*There is only dexterity where I wanted
firmness* — to forbid the leafing
colors of emotion, until one's face is stone.

THE WATCHMAN

Jasper Johns, 1964

On this wall of monitors, on one plane,
there's nowhere to hide in his circular world.

To the east, his view extends to the sea.
To the west, north, south, as far as one may be

looking back at him. Promoted, commended,
given the latitude to run things his way,

he detected the white incursion in a blizzard,
the black brigades on a moonless night.

How did we get clearance to be here,
to observe him observing? Here's my face

hanging on a chain around my neck,
though friends say they're unsure

about my motivation these days. They say
I'm not personal anymore. To quell the blur

of this touching confusion, a single screen,
small and dim, plays my home videos.

Here my brother and I are standing
along the line of lilacs, I pretend to instruct

on how to smell them properly.
Here are my daughters and birthday cakes,

my grandparents alive just before dying,
my wife stirring a can of paint.

And so the watchman takes his eyes
off the stretches of threatening spaces,

maybe my family disturbs him
in some vague way, maybe his own birthday

is approaching. But he has fallen
into the trap of looking,

he has forsaken his job and his pledge,
and despite the element of the personal,

the palsied half of my grandfather's face,
the watchman takes away no information.

THE INCENTIVE OF THE MAGGOT

The young nurses were summoned
by their mentor to examine gangrene.
Found on the living room floor

by her ex-husband, the patient was alcoholic,
abdomen septic, and now the extremities
were charred with rot. Unconscious,

systems stalling. The infection-fighting
drug caused blood, flowing to the organs,
to disregard the more distant pathways,

encouraging the gangrene. They make them look
at the uncurable, and struggle with the sense
of regimen, while we in the waiting room

wait for outcomes and the screen flashes
with the image of a small plane crashing,
then crashing again in slow motion,

a privately owned twin-engine tilting
at the runway cleared for its return.
Overheated room, everyone is nodding off.

Insurgents shot in Sri Lanka and Liberia.
Bones found nearby in the Neponset marshes.
So a young nurse, of a particular temperament,

may come to resent, may angrily refuse
to use grief for the purpose of edification.
She may feel contempt for a journalist's catalogue

of atrocities, genitals beaten with a ruler.
Not because they are not actual,
but because someone looked and discovered nothing.

Flavius Josephus described the infirmities
of Herod the Great: incessant itching,
excruciating intestinal pain, breathlessness,

convulsions in every limb, rotting
of the genitalia. The brains behind
the Slaughter of the Innocents died of gangrene

in his penis and kidneys, says the voiceover.
Fournier's gangrene, a rare variety.
But we will not have to look at the coffins

of our dead soldiers. They will not let us
gaze on their coffins, in transit.
Praise for the edict that will not permit

videotape to roll over the suddenly dead.
Praise for this moment of pause, of darkness,
of refusal to look at anything other

than the final report of the doctor on call,
the process of discreetly removing a corpse.
Not long ago I sat with a clairvoyant;

she said in my past life
I was slain on an English battlefield.
But others were saved by green blowflies,

their larvae made a soup in the gashes and rips,
dressed the wounds and farmed our flesh.
The survivors lay in a drowse of pain.

Timelessly they stirred, rose up, staggered in boots
and quickened their steps, as if they had discarded
the dead parts of themselves.

ONE FIREFLY

He is waiting to be seen.
In this world I hardly matter.

What goes into the dark
to be seen? Nothing like me.

There is a festival of fireflies
in Muju-gun in August

where people pray for firefly prosperity,
in Korea, since the Japanese

exterminated their fireflies
experimenting with insecticides.

Firefly is a Japanese idea.
The one in my yard lives alone.

To be so solitary while signaling
for love, to be content knowing

the night has no real presences
except for the one who makes himself

their flickering mirror. Who ignites
and diminishes as they would.

How do we lose a lovely idea?
Desperate we don't count.

Who wouldn't prefer a fullness of fireflies
in their habitat? The males

flying while they flash for the females
who wait in the tall grass and flash back.

The fullness is one idea.
The idea must not matter

so that one firefly suffices for a thousand years.
The entomologists take us further.

They ask us to reflect
that the firefly is not a true fly. It is a beetle.

"RITORNA-ME"

Open the gate for me
at the hour of the closing of the gate.

Caretaker, childhood friend, you must hear
many unreasonable requests in this time
of broken speech. What's left us
but to approach?

An old woman spoke to me in the supermarket:
I don't know where the jam is anymore.
We found seven brands of blueberry jam,
she reached for one indifferently
and asked, *What's the name of that song?*
I knew the answer, just as you respond,

Crocosmia, the hybrid called Lucifer
when they ask, *What's that stunning red flower*
captivating the hummingbird?

You and I used to find everything
worthy of our best banter.
So if I say, Beyond the cloaking row of spruces
is a world that exaggerates itself,
a city disengaged from its harbor
but wearing a sailor's cap rakishly,
city of costly penury and parades,
votes cast, lots picked, justice expected —

if I say this, are we unchanged?
Once I complained that so much had been kept
from me, and then I caught on.

The crab crawls sideways on the disused beach
and the wind follows him exactly.

How did you become the one who tends
this ravished garden with the sun angling
behind the spruces along with starlings?
It's a fool who yearns
for his native city — when Odysseus returned
only his nurse recognized him

and she had changed much more than he.
I've come back out of the necessity to finish.
For the distance of this season,
fifty days from leaf-flare to leaf-fall,
I've asked, Why was I absent and silent

for so many years? Then answered:
This was the difficulty I wanted, to go
deeper where the details are quiet,
like cobblestones beside the cathedral of Cologne
at a very late hour, and the cathedral itself,
a day of tiresome transactions ahead.

Because she couldn't find her jam
I was moved to see your face again —
twice its memory has appeared
in the faces of women I wouldn't love.
An unremarkable story.
                           And during its telling
your garden has become too dark to appreciate
and my face unfamiliar.

FROM THE CITY OF REFUGE

There's no point blaming an anthill
when there's no sugar in the pantry.
Time has stolen the sugar, meaning
for years we ate like thieves.

The cities of menace are invaded precisely,
the killings are inadvertent,
as if soldiers aren't fighting but hauling
tons of crushed rock that spill by mistake,

gravel animated by a blown tire, by God,
flung with an outpouring like applause
onto whoever shouldn't have been in the way.

There's no point in taking a corporal's life,
so we call it the guilty act of an innocent
and send him here to the city of refuge,
a place of little commerce
so as not to attract his blood avenger.

Back home they pray for a messiah
to save the good and savage the bad.
Here we say there's no point.
Not that we see beyond or through evil,
but that we can't be overwhelmed
by the inadvertent bad in who we are.

I once stole from a faceless institution
until it turned around and found me.
We were lugging out sacks of sugar,
I dropped one from a murderous height.

What a relief when it's not me
who meets up with his avenger.

Here I have everything for a life,
steady employment, parks for pleasure,
everything but a ration of sugar,
which I no longer crave.

There's a boulder in the Japanese garden
for contemplation of a boulder's noble mass
and its inner identity as a load of stone.

The avenger has no way in
but he may already be inside.
On the horizon, I see the dim glow
from the cities of no return.

WHAT WAS NORMAL

When the meteor shower ends,
a constellation like a hearse

will pick us up and take us to bed.
Next time this happens we'll be dead.

We spin to pass through old debris,
bits as small as a bitten nail

flare to enter our wintry night.
How pathetic to know the waste

even in the fortunate career of a comet,
its isolation in an intimate system.

At the whipping end of the comet's tail
a new notion of our past lives sets in,

a dream of a perfect moment passed.
We are filled, while watching the night sky,

with admiration for the stealth
of Orion, armed to his steely teeth,

infiltrating distant dens when we sleep.
He swats away a last epochal ember.

But there are some who recall the sinister
recurrence of rhubarb, chestnuts, and jam.

A coffee made of barley juice and saccharine,
bistros stripped of copper counters.

Stores without suppliers,
farms without pickers.

Invaders ruining the harvest.
First their strange presence,

then the strange absences.
People vanishing en masse, flaring out.

Henri Bergson shuffling through the streets
in his carpet slippers, lecturing on laughter.

I feel as if I remember all of this.
I feel as if it's our last chance to recall

the conventions of normal tough times.
Because now we're safe to side

against ourselves, our sparkling thoughts
are shooting into the space of their speaking

where Orion gazes through night-vision goggles
and what formerly was normal is a carbonized wisp.

TRISTIA AT NEAP TIDE

This is the bottom
of an ocean in retreat.
The flats are fingered with ridges
where water lost its grip and slid away.
This is a day when the voice of the sea
falls back silent in its throat and I must think
of myself. There is the possibility of walking out
farther than ever, no shingle or wrack
to impede the way, no crabs entrenched
in the mud for birth-giving, no mackerel
driven aground bleeding by hungering bluefish,
no rusting objects. The moon clenches.
Nothing gives way, having already given,
whatever must end will end
later, sand dunes collect themselves,
a salt marsh inhales its newly apparent
stench, an estuary cracks open its skin
for sunlight to trickle into the gaps.
An onshore wind chases after the absent sea.
You asked me to show you the expansive life,
here it is. I asked you for news of the state —
why? Because I prefer my exile
to occur during critical times,
hospital ships leaving the unsiltable harbor.
You asked me to predict how far
this rippled sweep would go. Evading you,
I turned my vision into a veering tern's.
What I discovered abased me.
Buried like a bivalve, *Venus mercenaria,*
I took your full weight
when you stood above me to gaze at the expanse.

But now we've made our farewells,
the gulls find nothing of value
in the shallow tidepools so they recline,
facing the westering sun.
It is true I am a self-banisher.
I won't endeavor to dispense advice
or excuse my bad manners —
but the smell of an invisible ocean
lasts forever. What I do to the image
of a sea somewhere digesting its own black bilge
is more important to me than what that image
does to my salt-caked brain. I will
go further: I take full responsibility
for the ephemeral daring presence
of a shard of wave-smooth amber glass at my feet.
May God and the emperor save the thoughtless walker,
encircled by safe land in turn surrounded
by the removed sea.
I do not know where to go next
since no one anticipates me.
But the space, it opens up.

TURBULENT FERRY, EVENING

To spend one's stored power
keeping watch, taking responsibility
for the wanton and the dull.
Mainland to island and back.

In these mythic rips, a myopic yacht drifts
until the force cleaves it exactly
midships, in a lacy mist.

To ease into the slip
so many times in a lifetime
that the act becomes imponderable.
So ingrained in its restraint
like a future saint moving into marble.

After the stern door cranks down
and a ballast of breath debarks,
the ferry feels a great peace
it doesn't have, spreading in light chop,
in the chilling autumn soundwater.

Because the island blinks in demand,
because the ferry has no serenity,
in vigilance it knots a dim pleasure
supposing such calmness exists.

"Crow Menace in Tokyo": In September 2001, the Earth Environment Service reported that 21,000 crows had migrated to Tokyo from the jungles of southeast Asia. The Tokyo city government vowed to eliminate them.

"End of the Peacock Throne": Leila Pahlavi, youngest daughter of the late shah of Iran, died from an overdose of sleeping pills on June 9, 2001, in Paris. She was thirty-one.

"Hermaphrodite Endormi": The sculpture is displayed in the Louvre. Roman, sculptor unknown, circa A.D. 200.

"Warm Canto": An early draft of the poem mentioned and was titled after Mal Waldron's jazz piece "Warm Canto," featuring Eric Dolphy, on the 1961 album *The Quest*. I kept the title.

"Monuments": Käthe Kollwitz sculpted two figures (*The Parents*) to commemorate the German military cemetery at Roggevelde in Belgium. Her son, Peter, was killed in the first week of fighting at Ypres in 1914. The pieces were not installed until 1932.

"The Watchman": The painting by Jasper Johns. He stated that the watchman is equated with the spectator of art who "falls into the trap of looking, leaves his job, and takes away no information."

"The Incentive of the Maggot": Lines in the eighth stanza adapt words written by Robert Frost on the death of Edward Thomas: "Something in me refuses to take the risk—angrily refuses to take the risk—of seeming to use grief for literary purposes."

"'Ritorna-Me'": This is the title of a 1958 recording by Dean Martin. It reached number four on the *Billboard* pop chart.

"From the City of Refuge": Six cities in ancient Israel were designated in Numbers 35:1–34 as cities of refuge, established to protect the accidental slayer from the revenge of the offended family.

ACKNOWLEDGMENTS

With care and candor, Louise Glück worked with me over the course of a year to improve my manuscript and open the way to new poems that completed this book.

Floyd Skloot read and critiqued these poems as they emerged. Thank you, Floyd, for thirty years of friendship.

Thank you, Robert Pinsky, for selecting my manuscript for the Bakeless Prize.

Special thanks to Dave Clewell, Donna and George Disario, Paul Fraser, Bill Hamilton, Arnost Lustig, Craig Moodie, Carol and Leonard Nathan, and Aki and Hammett Nurosi for their ideas and support.

The italicized lines in "Monuments" are taken from the diary of Käthe Kollwitz, entries dated December 21, 1926 and October 22, 1929, as published in *The Diary and Letters of Käthe Kollwitz*, Northwestern University Press, 1988.

"The Plan for Cyprus" is dedicated to Swanee Hunt and Charles Ansbacher.

I am grateful to the editors of the following magazines, in which some of these poems first appeared: "Crow Menace in Tokyo," "One Firefly," and "Tristia at Neap Tide," *TriQuarterly;* "The Demise of Camembert," "Shame," and "Warm Canto," *Slate;* "The Final Call" and "Light Fingers," *The New Yorker;* and "Safe Passage," *The Threepenny Review*.

BREAD LOAF AND THE BAKELESS PRIZES

The Katharine Bakeless Nason Literary Publication Prizes were established in 1995 to expand Bread Loaf Writers' Conference's commitment to the support of emerging writers. Endowed by the LZ Francis Foundation, the prizes commemorate the Middlebury College patron Katharine Bakeless Nason and launch the publication career of a poet, fiction writer, and creative nonfiction writer annually. Winning manuscripts are chosen in an open national competition by a distinguished judge in each genre. Winners are published by Houghton Mifflin Company in Mariner paperback original.

2004 JUDGES

Robert Pinsky, poetry

Charles Baxter, fiction

William Kittredge, creative nonfiction